W is for Wind

A Weather Alphabet

Written by Pat Michaels and Illustrated by Melanie Rose

Text Copyright © 2005 Pat Michaels
Illustration Copyright © 2005 Melanie Rose

Sleeping Bear Press™

315 E. Eisenhower Parkway, Ste. 200
Ann Arbor, MI 48108
www.sleepingbearpress.com

Sleeping Bear Press is an imprint of Gale, a part of Cengage Learning.

10 9 8 7 6 5 4 3 2 1 (case)
10 9 8 7 6 5 4 3 (pbk)

Library of Congress Cataloging-in-Publication Data

Paulauski, Patrick.
W is for wind : a weather alphabet / written by Pat Michaels;
illustrated by Melanie Rose.
p. cm.
Summary: "An A-Z pictorial for children including weather terms such as barometer, cloud, tornado, and sunshine introduced with poems accompanied by expository text to provide detailed information"—Provided by publisher.

pbk ISBN-13: 978-1-58536-330-8   case ISBN-13: 978-1-58536-237-0

1. Weather—Juvenile literature. 2. Alphabets—Juvenile literature. I. Rose, Melanie, ill. II. Title.
QC981.3.P38 2005
428.1'3—dc22   2004027294

Printed by China Translation & Printing Services Limited,
Guangdong Province, China. 3rd printing.   10/2011

A a

The atmosphere is like a great ocean surrounding the Earth. But our atmosphere isn't water. It is made up of gases that are constantly moving and without it, the Earth could not support life. One of the most important gases in the atmosphere is oxygen, even though the atmosphere contains mostly nitrogen.

There are four layers in the atmosphere. The troposphere contains almost all of the gases that allow us to breathe and is always moving and shifting about, causing changes in our weather. The stratosphere extends from about seven to 30 miles (11.3–48.3 km) above the Earth with air so thin that no person could breathe. Few airplanes can fly in this layer. The mesosphere is where the temperature can be -90 degrees Fahrenheit (-67.8°C). This layer is about 50 miles (80.5 km) high, much higher than most airplanes can fly. Special helium balloons, high-altitude planes and rockets can reach this altitude. The highest layer, the thermosphere or ionosphere, extends to the edge of space and temperatures can be between 900 and 3,000 degrees Fahrenheit (482.2–1648.9°C).

A is for Atmosphere.

Rivers of air flow around the Earth every day.
It gives us the oxygen we need to live and play.
The winds constantly shift and move from place to place.
They bring the gentle breezes you feel upon your face.

Have you ever heard the expression "under the weather"? Guess what? We are all "under the weather." An instrument called the barometer measures the weight of our atmosphere above our heads. Some days the atmosphere is taller and weighs more. And sometimes it is shorter and is lighter. These are small changes that the barometer measures. The tall, heavy atmosphere causes high pressure and usually brings dry, sunny weather. Low-pressure systems indicate a lighter atmosphere, bringing rain and sometimes very stormy weather. The change in the barometric pressure over time is a very good indicator of the coming changes in the weather.

In the United States the barometric readings are commonly reported in inches. The most common, average reading is around 30. Most other countries measure pressure using the metric system in millibars. Thirty inches of mercury would equal about 1,015 millibars. Meteorologists around the world, including the United States use millibar measurements for atmospheric readings.

Evangelista Torricelli, an assistant of Galileo, the famous Italian astronomer, invented the barometer almost 400 years ago.

B is for Barometer.

As our atmosphere grows larger and smaller,
the barometer will become shorter and taller.
The long tube of mercury will show the measure,
always sensing the weight of the air pressure.

C is for Cloud.

Sometimes they are puffy and white
and they make animal shapes that delight,
but clouds have a more serious role.
Some contain rain that makes the plants grow.

Clouds are the water buckets of the world, and everything that lives and grows depends on them. They are made up of water droplets that are so small they float. Sometimes those droplets form bigger droplets and fall as rain. High clouds, called cirrus clouds, are made mostly of ice crystals. Lower clouds that cover large areas are called stratus. Fog is a type of stratus cloud and forms from high humidity near the ground. Cumulus clouds are white, fluffy ones you might see against a bright blue sky. Sometimes these clouds build up and make shapes, and then fall apart. Cumulus clouds can become very tall and turn dark, and can collect so much water that they will become a rain cloud. When these clouds form into thunderstorms, they become cumulonimbus clouds, reaching very high in the atmosphere, sometimes 50 to 60 thousand feet (15.2 km–18.3 km). Storms that high can cause severe weather with high winds, frequent lightning, hail, and tornadoes.

D is for Dew.

Gentle droplets form on the leaves and grass.
Morning turns cool and still as the hours pass.
Water becomes thick and coats the tall trees.
Dew drips from the cups of the water-filled leaves.

Have you ever heard the weather reporter talk about the dew point? That point is really a temperature. When the temperature falls overnight, the air around us becomes cool and very humid. The cool air causes the water in the air, called water vapor, to become visible when it collects on the ground, on our cars, or even on a playground swing. This process is called condensation. The dew disappears in the daylight hours, when the sun raises the temperature. The water evaporates again and becomes water vapor.

D is also for dust devil. Summer heat can rise so rapidly that it swirls in an upward spiral. A dust devil acts like a small tornado, picking up dust, leaves, and trash and swirling them in the air, but they are not tornadoes. Usually the hot column of air won't last very long, giving dust devils a short life span.

Evaporation is the reverse of the formation of dew. When the air warms, it causes the water on the ground or anywhere else to disappear. Actually, it just turns back into the invisible water called vapor. Sometimes you can see evaporation working its magic on hot summer days after a rain shower. The water turns into steam and rises into the air. The steam will disappear into the air as water vapor. Evaporation is part of the process called the water cycle. Sooner or later in that cycle, the water will become visible again, during condensation when clouds and dew form.

E is for Evaporation.

The summer steam rises from an afternoon shower.
The ground is almost dry within an hour.
And where does the water go from there?
It disappears and goes back into the air.

E e

F f

F is for Funnel cloud.

Sometimes clouds become fierce and dark.
They fill with water and begin to spark.
They spin like tops around and around.
We call them tornadoes when they touch the ground.

When a thunderstorm becomes severe, strong winds can rotate from a column of air. That column will reach down from the thunderstorm to become a funnel cloud. These very strong, rotating winds contain water droplets from the storm that cause the funnel cloud to become visible. If a funnel cloud reaches the ground, it is called a tornado. When the tornado reaches or forms over water, we call it a waterspout.

Frost is another word that begins with **F**. Remember dew? Well, frost is the frozen version of dew. The same process called condensation causes frost to form. The only difference is that the temperature has to fall to the freezing point, 32 degrees Fahrenheit (0°C), or below in order for a frost to occur.

Mr. Fahrenheit, Gabriel, that is, invented the first mercury thermometer in 1724.

G is for Glacier.

The trenches are marked by a large ice form
where highlands once stood, now valleys are born.
The glaciers slide south during the years of cold.
The landscape takes shape from the large ice mold.

If you thought you had a lot of ice in your refrigerator, think how much is contained in the world's glaciers. These large bodies of ice are found all over the world in mountainous areas, as well as the polar regions. Some glaciers grow larger and smaller with the changing of the seasons. But the polar glaciers usually stay the same size. The continent of Antarctica contains the world's largest ice sheet. If all the ice from Antarctica were melted, it would supply the Mississippi River with flowing water for more than 50,000 years.

G is also for greenhouse effect. As our Earth travels through cold space, it is constantly bathed in warm sunlight, which can produce heat buildup in our atmosphere. The Earth radiates that heat back into space. The collection of gases like carbon dioxide and methane keeps much of the heat from escaping. The greenhouse effect is credited with keeping the Earth's average temperature about 60 degrees Fahrenheit (15.6°C) warmer than it would otherwise be.

H is for Hurricane.

The winds swirl around in a large formation.
Storms of this size need no magnification.
Meteorologists study them with eyes from space.
For some, the storm is something to chase.

Hurricanes are among the biggest storms on Earth, and they contain some of the strongest winds. Hurricanes form above the warm ocean waters. They start out as a small area of thunderstorms, and continue to grow, first into a tropical wave, then into a tropical depression, meaning it will start to circulate in an organized weather system. When the tropical system contains winds that are constant or sustained at 39 miles (62.8 km) per hour or more, it becomes a named tropical storm. The system is upgraded to a hurricane when the winds are sustained at 74 miles (119.1 km) per hour or more. Satellites can show us these monster storms, some 300 miles (482.8 km) wide.

Hurricanes are rated in their intensity and wind speed by the Saffir-Simpson rating scale and range from category one to category five. A category one hurricane has winds from 74 to 95 miles (119.1–152.9 km) per hour, and causes damage to some trees and shrubbery. A category five hurricane contains winds of 155 miles (249.4 km) per hour or greater and homes and small buildings can be completely destroyed.

The magical temperature is 32 degrees Fahrenheit, or 0 degrees Celsius. Our wonderful world of water begins to freeze and take on a new form, a solid. Also at this freezing temperature precipitation turns from rain to freezing rain or into snow. Are any two snowflakes shaped exactly alike? The answers is, no. When you look closely with a microscope, you can see that they are all different.

Ice age also begins with I. The largest ice age occurred around 650,000 years ago, when ice glaciers covered the Northern Hemisphere and dug as far south as central Indiana. This ice age lasted about 50,000 years. It was followed by smaller ice ages, each about 100,000 years apart.

The last of the ice ages was officially named the Ice Age, and it peaked about 20,000 years ago. Our Earth has been slowly warming since our last ice age. Our modern-day weather has been described as global warming which continues to this day. Many years in the future, we may see another ice age.

I i

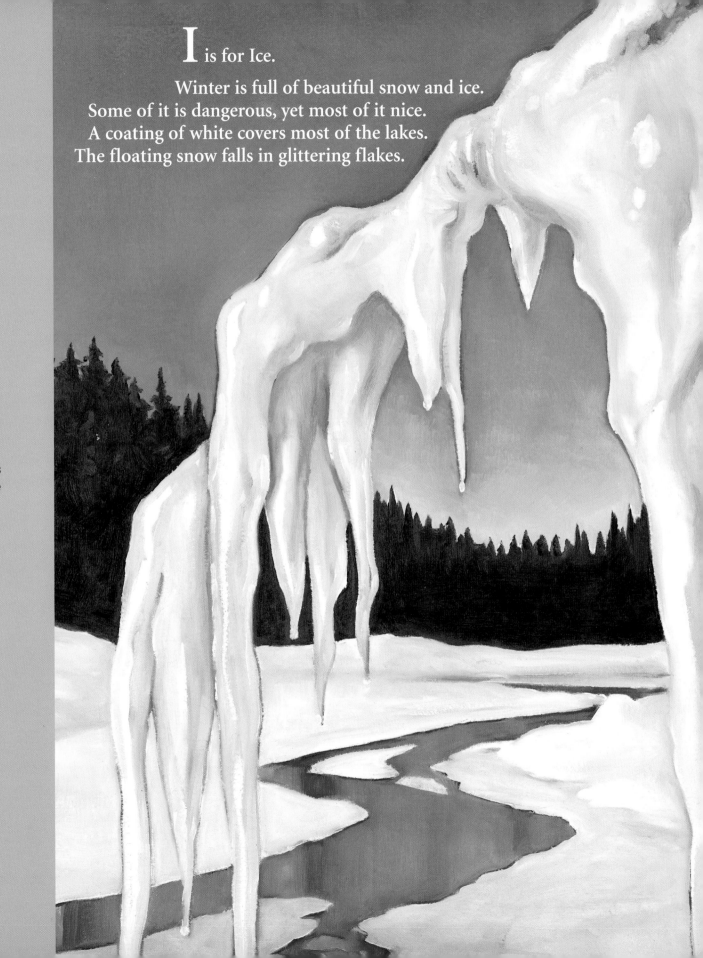

I is for Ice.

Winter is full of beautiful snow and ice.
Some of it is dangerous, yet most of it nice.
A coating of white covers most of the lakes.
The floating snow falls in glittering flakes.

J j

Like a river of air, the jet stream moves rapidly high in the atmosphere, speeding up and slowing down. It will move north and then south, causing our weather to change. The jet stream's movement affects weather patterns in the lower atmosphere. It is called jet stream because it flows very fast, sometimes more than 100 miles (160.9 km) per hour.

You can catch a ride in a jet stream by flying through it in an airplane. Sometimes it can cause a bumpy ride, or it can give an airplane a boost by giving the plane a "tail" wind. There can be several jet streams at any time in the United States or Canada. There are northern jets streams that bring cold weather into southern states. When a jet stream makes a sudden turn south and then north, the weather will usually change quickly. Sometimes these sudden shifts can cause severe weather.

J is for Jet Stream.

The jet stream has a really fast name.
It keeps the weather from being the same.
North and south it makes the air flow.
With its constant changing, it makes our weather go.

You may have heard an airplane pilot give his speed in knots. Why? We can thank the mariners who have steered their ships through turbulent seas. Wind is measured in miles-per-hour over land. But over the sea and in the air, we measure wind in knots. One knot is a little more than one mile-per-hour. Knots are used to measure wind speeds recorded by measuring devices called buoys. The word "knot" comes from "nautical." A nautical mile is a little longer than a mile measured on land, about 1.15 miles to be exact. The measurement is used in marine navigation, and is some-times called sea miles.

K is also for the Kelvin temperature scale. Can you imagine a freezing temperature of 273 degrees? That is the freezing point for the Kelvin scale. And the boiling point is 100 degrees higher, at 373 degrees. Scientists use the scale for studying the effects of extreme temperatures on substances. And if you thought the Kelvin scale is named after someone, you're right. It was named after William T. Kelvin, a Scottish physicist and mathematician.

K k

K is for Knots.

If the wind blows, mariners give it a different name,
not measured in miles, but almost the same.
Sailors know they should take heed,
to adjust their sails for maximum speed.

L l

L is for Lightning.

Dancing across the nighttime sky
lightning is reflected in your eye.
Its power seems somewhat of a mystery.
If we could catch it, we might change history.

An average lightning bolt is five times hotter than the surface of the sun and one strike is hot enough to turn sand into glass. Since the sun's temperature is around 6,000 degrees Fahrenheit (3315.6°C), that makes the average bolt of lightning around 30,000 degrees (16648.9°C). The discharge from a bolt causes a shock wave that we hear as thunder.

Lightning can strike from a cloud to the ground or from a cloud to another cloud. Sometimes lightning will strike into the air. Forked lightning is the most common type, striking thousands of feet from a cloud to the ground. Sheet lightning causes clouds to glow because it is lightning inside the clouds. Ball lightning is a very rare type that seems to break away from a bolt and travel across the ground before dissipating. Another very fascinating type of lightning is called St. Elmo's fire. It causes radio antennas, airplane wings, and power poles to light up with sparks traveling into the air. Some people have described it as a fiery glow.

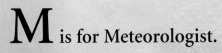

M is for Meteorologist.

How will we know what tomorrow may bring?
The weather is constantly changing everything.
It's a serious challenge to say it will rain.
Especially when there is much to lose or gain.

Do you remember Benjamin Franklin's weather studies? He flew a kite into the air to measure electricity. If you study the weather or take readings of the atmosphere, you are also a meteorologist. You can be an amateur meteorologist or one who has taken years of meteorology college courses.

Understanding this complicated science includes knowledge of many other sciences like oceanography, geography, mathematics, and physics. Meteorologists work in all types of industries, including aviation and agriculture.

Some meteorologists are the weather forecasters you see each day on television. These forecasters put together computer graphics using satellite and radar images to tell viewers how the weather will affect them. Many television forecasters stand in front of a large screen, with the weather graphics added behind them during the broadcast in a computerized process called color or chroma keying. The weather graphics look as if they are actually behind the weather person. Doing the weather in front of a chroma key wall can sometimes be tricky, since the television meteorologist is actually pointing to a blank wall.

M
m

N n

N is for Northern Lights.

The colors that dance through the northern sky
make the heart jump with sheer joy to the eye.
The solar winds brush gently past the Earth
and make the skies glow, giving a delightful mirth.

They have been described as curtains of light and are one of the natural wonders of the world. The best place to view the northern lights is in northern climates, closer to the North Pole. The sun gives off high-energy particles called solar wind that strike the Earth. These particles strike the Earth's outer atmosphere called the ionosphere, causing them to react with the Earth's magnetic field. This causes the particles to glow in colors like red, green, blue, and violet.

The northern lights appear to dance across the sky. The northern lights are also called the aurora borealis. "Aurora" means "lights," and "borealis" means "northern." The lights seen in the southern hemisphere are called the southern lights or aurora australis.

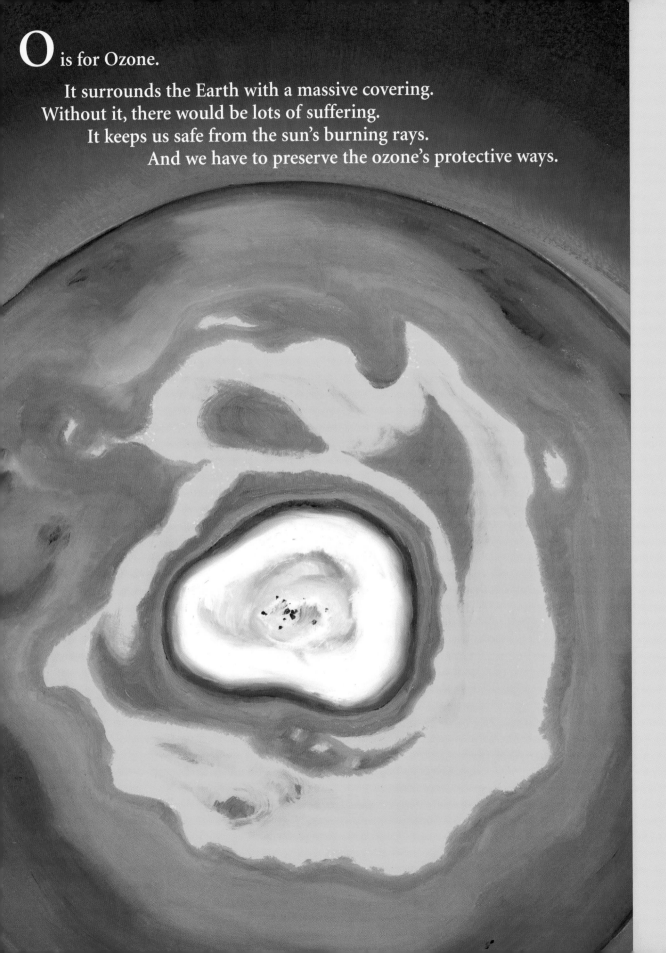

O is for Ozone.

It surrounds the Earth with a massive covering.
Without it, there would be lots of suffering.
It keeps us safe from the sun's burning rays.
And we have to preserve the ozone's protective ways.

Ozone occurs naturally in the stratosphere, the outer part of the atmosphere. It serves as a large protective covering around the world. It prevents the sun's harmful ultra-violet rays from reaching us.

The ozone layer has become very thin in places, especially at the Earth's North and South Poles. Studies have found that certain chemicals used in refrigeration and air-conditioning were harming the ozone layer. Since that study, efforts to reduce production of the harmful chemicals may be successful in protecting the blanket of air that protects us.

Oo

Pp

Precipitation can take many different forms. Rain can fall as a mist, small sprinkles, or even large drops during thunderstorms. During the hot summer months, severe thunderstorms can produce hail when a storm builds so high in the atmosphere that the water droplets freeze. Hail can be very devastating, stripping leaves from trees, denting cars, and breaking glass.

Rain occurs in the winter as freezing rain. The water turns to ice when it makes contact with the ground or objects. Winter precipitation can also come in the form of sleet, a combination of rain, snow, and an icy mix. Graupel and ice pellets are other types of frozen precipitation that fall during the winter months.

P is also for poles. The North Pole and the South Pole are extreme ends of the world. During the winter at the South Pole, the sun never rises. It is dark all day! That is why the temperatures can be some of the coldest on Earth, averaging -50 degrees Fahrenheit (-45.6°C).

Pis for Precipitation.

Sometimes it falls in a gentle shower.
But thunderstorms offer much more power.
In winter it falls as snow or sleet.
And rain that freezes on the street.

It is a saying in just about every part of the world, "If you don't like the weather, just wait a minute. It'll change." In some places, that fact is true. Cold fronts usually cause the most changes. They can drop the temperature in your neighborhood, as winds blast through within just a few minutes. The atmospheric pressure can change drastically, causing some people to feel the change in the weather. Quick changes can cause severe weather, bringing heavy storms and even tornadoes.

One of the quickest changes in the United States occurred on January 23 and 24, 1916. In Browning, Montana the temperature dropped nearly 100 degrees Fahrenheit (37.8°C), from 44 above 0 to 56 below 0 (6.7 to -48.9°C). That quick change was caused by arctic air that swept into Montana.

Q is for Quick weather changes.

The wind turns around with the blink of an eye.
The temperature drops and clouds fill the sky.
Weather instruments swing wildly, going forward and back.
As the storm approaches, satellite and radar watch its track.

You can thank Roy G. Biv for helping us remember the colors of the rainbow. Actually, he is not a real man. The letters in his name come from red, orange, yellow, green, blue, indigo, and violet. The colors of the rainbow always fall in that order.

Light from the sun strikes raindrops and it is refracted. That means the light is bent into different angles. When light is bent, its colors show through. Do you think you'll ever find the end of a rainbow?

R is for Rainbow.

When sunlight shines on the rain just right
     it gives us a most beautiful, colorful sight.
It inspires a promise of hope and love—
     a message that seems to come from above.

S is for Sunshine.

The sand reflects the warmth on your face.
A breeze carries sounds of a summer place.
Buckets of seashells dry in the bright light.
Children splash through the water with delight.

Florida is commonly called the Sunshine State. But it isn't at the top of the sunny list. Arizona is really the sunshine state, if you consider how much sunshine it gets. Yuma, Arizona just so happens to be the sunniest place on Earth. Let's talk hours here. If Yuma never saw a cloud it would have nearly 4,500 hours of sunshine each year. It actually has about 4,000. How does Florida fare on the sunshine meter? Orlando, which lies in the middle of the state, receives about 3,000 sunshine hours a year.

Keeping tabs of the total amount of sunshine a year can be valuable. Sunshine provides a renewable source of energy that can be stored and used to power homes, buildings, and even streetlights. Solar panels contain cells that turn sunshine into electrical power that can be stored in batteries. Those batteries then provide the electricity needed to power lights and appliances, even cars. Solar power is a renewable, clean source of energy, but scientists haven't developed a very efficient process of collecting it. A yard full of solar panels wouldn't provide enough energy to power everything we use in our homes, like air-conditioning, computers, and large screen televisions.

S s

T is for Tornado.

From the storm's bottom, the funnel cloud is attached.
The tornado's wind power on Earth is unmatched.
The twister can make long marks on the land below.
Sometimes destroying homes, such sadness it can bestow.

Tt

It is one of the most fascinating forces in nature, and people who have seen tornadoes never forget them. Meteorologists are just now beginning to understand some of the mysteries surrounding these almost unpredictable, devastating twisters.

Tornadoes are classified by the Fujita scale, invented by Ted Fujita, a meteorologist and professor, who was driven to find out the mysteries of the world's strongest winds. The first part of the scale, F-0 starts at around 78 miles (125.5 km) per hour. The top part of the scale is F-5, which classifies tornadoes with winds near 300 miles (482.8 km) per hour.

This spinning column of air, in rare cases, can produce winds that can reach over 300 miles (482.8 km) per hour, and they can cause tremendous damage. But most tornadoes are much weaker, and skip across the ground. A tornado that has not reached the ground is called a funnel cloud. A tornado over a lake, sea, or the ocean is called a waterspout.

U is for Umbrella.

They pop up like mushrooms after a spring rain.
Wet city streets transform into a colorful train.
A parade of umbrellas, each one a different size.
Still the confusion of whose is whose is no surprise.

Invented more than 4,000 years ago, the earliest umbrella was first designed to protect us from the sun, yet nowadays most umbrellas are sold on rainy days. The word "umbrella" comes from the Latin root word "umbra," meaning shade or shadow.

It is believed that the Chinese were the first to use umbrellas as rain protection. Umbrellas were also called parasols, and wax and lacquer was used as a coating to keep out the rain.

Did you know the umbrella is the item people lose most often?

U u

V is for Vapor.

It flows in the wind, a gas invisible to the eye.
It doesn't look like water until we see it in the sky.
Cloud's droplets form from the vapor we can't see,
sometimes on the lawn or a cool glass of tea.

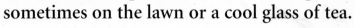

It's all around us, and we can't see it or smell it. A large room could contain a gallon of the colorless gas called water vapor. Water as a liquid also exists on Earth as a solid when it freezes into ice, or as a gas, when it becomes water vapor.

We say it is humid when the air contains a lot of water vapor. We can actually see water vapor in the air when it becomes fog or clouds. This process is called condensation, which turns vapor into small water droplets. Sometimes the vapor will form on objects, often during the nighttime hours. We can wake up and see the results when dew or frost forms from thin air.

W is for Wind.

It flows south, north, east, and west.
The wind is never really at rest.
The world depends on its constant ebb and flow.
Without wind the weather would have nowhere to go.

If we didn't have wind, the weather would never change. The constant movement of air stirs up the atmosphere. The wind can blow from any direction, even up or down, and it is described by the direction from which it blows. A northwest wind comes from the northwest, and is headed to the southeast.

Winds are categorized by the Beaufort scale, invented by Rear Admiral Sir Francis Beaufort in 1805. He was an Irish commander who devised the wind force scale for warships sailing on the ocean.

The scale ranges from 1 to 12, with 1 representing a light wind, and 12 being hurricane-force winds.

A gale force wind is just one example on the Beaufort scale with winds from 32 to 63 miles (51.5–101.4 km) per hour. Some winds can be much faster and stronger.

W
W

X is for X-rays.

The rays stream from our sun like light.
But they can't be seen in anyone's sight.
Its cosmic radiation can cause severe pain,
but in the right kind of doses, can be quite tame.

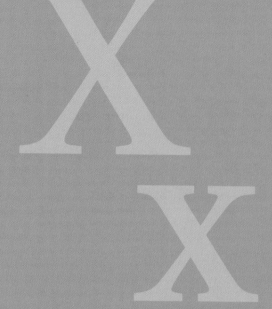

Some X-rays come from our sun. They are a type of light, but you cannot see them. X-rays travel through solid objects like our bodies, but they are harmless in the small amounts that come from the sun, because our atmosphere protects us.

X is also for X-band Doppler Radar. Doppler radar has significantly changed weather forecasting. Radio signals sweep across the land searching for precipitation. The X-band Doppler hunts for snow and can find the movement of the smallest flakes. This specialized radar is so sensitive it can even see wind blowing in clear air.

The "X" in the name is the letter given to the frequency of the signal that the radar uses to detect precipitation. The wavelengths transmitted by this type of radar are very small, about 2.5 centimeters, which allows it to see small water droplets of snowflakes. The wavelengths for other types of radars are much larger. The "L" band has a wavelength between 15 to 30 centimeters.

In one year the Earth makes one trip around the sun. This trip takes 365 days. During this cosmic circle around the sun, the Earth stays tilted so that we experience the change of seasons. When it is winter in the Southern Hemisphere, the north experiences summer, and vice versa.

During winter in the Northern Hemisphere, the Earth is tilted away from the sun. The sunlight strikes the ground at a very low angle, and the sun looks very low in the sky. This causes our weather to become colder. Antarctica has some of the coldest temperatures on Earth during winter. The coldest recorded temperature was recorded in Antarctica in 1983. The temperature dropped to a breath-freezing -128 degrees Fahrenheit (-88.9°C).

In the summer, the sunlight falls on the ground more directly, and the sun is very high in the sky. That is why the summers can be so hot. One of the hottest temperatures ever recorded occurred in Death Valley, California on July 10, 1913. The temperature rose to 134 degrees Fahrenheit (56.7°C).

Y y

Y is for Year.

Our world is turning and sailing through space.
Going around the sun at an incredible pace.
Caught in its solar circle of life called a year.
It's always dependable, with a schedule to adhere.

We might think that zero equals nothing. But when it comes to temperatures, zero is very important. It's the point at which water freezes in the Celsius scale, and it equals 32 degrees in the Fahrenheit scale. Water transforms into a solid form at this temperature. We see our weather change with the formation of snow, sleet and other forms of ice.

The Celsius scale was invented by Swedish Astronomer Anders Celsius. The boiling point on the Celsius scale is 100 degrees.

Z is also for Zulu Time, a funny sounding term that refers to the time measurement used by the military and for sciences like meteorology. The world is divided into 24 times zones. The "0" time zone starts in Greenwich, England, and works its way around the world in 24 sections. This 24-hour time-zone clock is used in communications, the military, international shipping, and computer operations. In zulu time, the next hour after the noon hour would be 13 hundred hours. Zulu time would continue on until 24 hundred hours, and then start over again at 00 hundred hours.

Z z

Z is for Zero.

Zero is very important in making our weather show.
The temperature at zero turns rain into snow.
Then, with the crossing of zero, back up mercury will go.
Say goodbye to the frozen ice and back to the water flow.

Pat Michaels

Lightning jumping from a 200-foot radio broadcast tower and dancing into the radio studio was enough to jumpstart Pat's career in weather. Born Patrick Michael Paulauski, he soon became Pat Michaels when his broadcasting career started. When he was just 15, Pat worked at a radio station in southern Georgia that was knocked off the air more than once by lightning.

As a meteorologist Pat has tracked many different kinds of storms, once reporting from the inside of Hurricane Bertha in Florida during a trip on a C-130 hurricane hunter plane. Following his 15-year career at WKMG in Orlando, Florida, Pat traded Florida thunderstorms for lake effect snow when he moved to Michigan. While the chief meteorologist at WLNS, a CBS television affiliate in Lansing, Michigan, Pat often watched the winter thaw give way to spring tornadoes and spent hours on air tracking their movements.

When Pat isn't on the air, he spends time talking to schoolchildren about weather and television forecasting and has always wanted to write about the power of weather. Pat currently resides in Orlando, Florida.

Melanie Rose

Melanie lives in Mississauga, Canada with her son Liam, and their two cats, Mickey and Meesha. *W is for Wind* is Melanie's sixth title with Sleeping Bear Press. She also illustrated *M is for Maple: A Canadian Alphabet*; *Z is for Zamboni: A Hockey Alphabet*; *K is for Kick: A Soccer Alphabet*; *H is for Home Run: A Baseball Alphabet*; and *The Gift of the Inuksuk*. Melanie is a graduate of the Ontario College of Art.